C++ DESIGN PATTERNS

AN OBJECT-ORIENTED PERSPECTIVE

OLIVER LUCAS JR

TABLE OF CONTENTS

Chapter 1

Chapter 2

Chapter 3

Chapter 4

Chapter 5

Chapter 6

Chapter 7

Chapter 8

Chapter 9

Chapter 10

Preface

Welcome to the world of object-oriented design in C++! This book, "C++ Design Patterns: An Object-Oriented Perspective," is your guide to mastering the art of building robust, maintainable, and elegant software using powerful design patterns.

In the ever-evolving landscape of software development, object-oriented programming (OOP) remains a cornerstone for creating complex yet manageable systems. C++, with its rich features and performance capabilities, is a language where OOP truly shines. But even with the best tools, crafting well-designed software requires more than just language proficiency; it demands an understanding of proven design principles and solutions.

That's where design patterns come in. They are reusable solutions to commonly occurring design problems, offering a time-tested approach to structuring your code, promoting flexibility, and ensuring maintainability. This book delves into the core principles of object-oriented design and explores a range of essential design patterns, all within the context of C++.

Whether you're a novice programmer just beginning your journey with C++ or an experienced developer looking to refine your skills, this book offers valuable insights and practical guidance. We'll start with the fundamentals of OOP, covering concepts like abstraction, encapsulation, inheritance, and polymorphism. Then, we'll dive into a variety of design patterns, from creational patterns like the Factory Method and Singleton to structural patterns like the Adapter and Decorator, and finally, behavioral patterns like the Observer and Strategy.

Each chapter provides clear explanations, illustrative examples, and real-world applications to solidify your understanding. You'll learn how to apply these patterns effectively in your C++ projects, writing code that is not only functional but also elegant, maintainable, and adaptable to change.

My aim is to equip you with the knowledge and tools to become a more proficient and confident C++ developer. By mastering the principles and patterns presented in this book, you'll be well-prepared to tackle complex software design challenges and create high-quality applications that stand the test of time.

So, let's embark on this journey together and unlock the power of object-oriented design in C++!

Chapter 1

Introduction to Object-Oriented Design

1.1 The Four Pillars of OOP

Object-oriented programming is a powerful way to structure your code, making it more organized, reusable, and easier to maintain. It's like building with LEGO bricks – you create individual pieces (objects) that can be combined and reused to build complex structures (programs).

At the heart of OOP are four key principles:

Abstraction: Hiding Complexity, Showing Essentials

Imagine you're driving a car. You use the steering wheel, pedals, and gear stick to control it, but you don't need to know about the intricate workings of the engine, transmission, and electronics under the hood. That's abstraction!

In OOP, abstraction means hiding the complex implementation details of an object and presenting only the essential information to the user.

This simplifies interaction with objects and makes code easier to understand and use.

Example in C++:

```
C++

class Car {
public:
```

```cpp
  void start();
  void accelerate();
  void brake();
private:
    // Complex engine and transmission details
hidden here
};
```

Encapsulation: Protecting Data, Controlling Access

Think of encapsulation as a protective capsule around your data. It keeps the data safe and allows controlled access through well-defined methods.

In OOP, encapsulation means bundling data and the methods that operate on that data within a single unit (the object).

This protects the data from accidental modification and ensures it's used correctly.

Example in C++:

C++

```cpp
class BankAccount {
private:
  double balance;
 public:
  void deposit(double amount);
  double getBalance();
};
```

Inheritance: Building on Existing Foundations

Inheritance is like creating a family tree for your objects. It allows you to create new objects (child classes) that inherit properties and behaviors from existing ones (parent classes).

This promotes code reuse and allows you to create specialized objects without starting from scratch.

Example in C++:

C++

```
class Animal {
public:
   void eat();
   void sleep();
};

class Dog : public Animal {
public:
   void bark();
};
```

Polymorphism: Many Forms, One Interface

Polymorphism means "many forms." In OOP, it allows objects of different classes to be treated as objects of a common type.

This enables you to write flexible and reusable code that can work with a variety of objects.

Example in C++:

C++

```
class Shape {
public:
   virtual void draw() = 0; // Abstract method
```

```cpp
};

class Circle : public Shape {
public:
  void draw() override;
};

class Square : public Shape {
public:
  void draw() override;
};
```

Why These Pillars Matter

These four pillars work together to create robust, maintainable, and scalable C++ programs. They enable you to:

Manage complexity: Break down large problems into smaller, more manageable objects.

Reuse code: Inherit and extend existing code to create new functionality.

Write flexible code: Create code that can adapt to changing requirements.

Improve code organization: Structure your code in a clear and logical way.

By mastering these principles, you'll be well on your way to becoming a proficient object-oriented C++ programmer!

1.2 Benefits of Object-Oriented Design

Object-oriented design (OOD) isn't just a theoretical concept; it brings tangible benefits to C++ programming and software development as a whole. Here's how it helps you write better code and build more robust systems:

Improved Code Organization and Structure

Modularity: OOD encourages breaking down complex systems into smaller, self-contained modules (classes and objects). This makes code easier to understand, navigate, and maintain.

Encapsulation: By bundling data and methods within objects, OOD promotes data hiding and protection, reducing the risk of accidental modification and improving code reliability.

Enhanced Code Reusability and Maintainability

Inheritance: OOD allows you to reuse existing code by creating new classes that inherit properties and behaviors from existing ones. This saves time and effort, promoting consistency and reducing redundancy.

Polymorphism: OOD enables you to write flexible code that can work with objects of different classes through a common interface, making it easier to adapt and extend your software.

Increased Productivity and Efficiency

Faster Development: Code reusability and modularity contribute to faster development cycles, allowing you to build software more efficiently.

Easier Debugging: Modular code makes it easier to identify and fix errors, as problems are often isolated within specific objects or classes.

Improved Collaboration: OOD promotes clear code organization and interfaces, making it easier for teams to collaborate on projects.

Real-World Benefits:

Reduced Development Costs: OOD can lead to lower development costs due to increased productivity, code reusability, and easier maintenance.

Improved Software Quality: OOD promotes robust, reliable, and maintainable software, leading to higher quality and fewer bugs.

Increased Scalability: OOD makes it easier to scale and adapt software to changing requirements and growing complexity.

Examples in C++:

Game Development: OOD is widely used in game development to represent game entities (characters, objects, environments) as classes with their own properties and behaviors.

GUI Applications: OOD is essential for building graphical user interfaces, where UI elements (buttons, windows, menus) can be represented as objects with their own functionalities.

Database Systems: OOD is used to model database entities and relationships, making it easier to manage and access data.

In Summary:

Object-oriented design in C++ empowers you to write code that is:

Organized and structured

Reusable and maintainable

Efficient and scalable

Robust and reliable

By embracing OOD principles, you can create high-quality software that meets the demands of modern applications.

1.3 Why Design Patterns Matter in C++

Design patterns aren't just abstract concepts; they're powerful tools that can significantly improve your C++ code and your overall approach to software design. Here's why they matter:

Solving Common Problems Elegantly

Proven Solutions: Design patterns provide tried-and-tested solutions to recurring design problems in object-oriented programming. They encapsulate the wisdom and experience of countless developers, offering you a head start in tackling common challenges.

Avoiding Reinventing the Wheel: Instead of spending time and effort devising solutions from scratch, you can leverage design patterns to apply proven approaches, saving time and reducing the risk of errors.

Improving Code Readability and Maintainability

Common Language: Design patterns provide a shared vocabulary for developers. When you use a well-known pattern, other developers instantly understand your intent and the structure of your code.

Easier Maintenance: Well-designed code using patterns is easier to understand, modify, and extend. This reduces maintenance costs and makes it easier to adapt your software to changing requirements.

Promoting Best Practices and Code Reusability

Encapsulation of Best Practices: Design patterns embody best practices in object-oriented design, promoting code that is modular, flexible, and robust.

Code Reusability: Many design patterns promote code reuse by encouraging the creation of reusable components and flexible structures. This reduces redundancy and improves consistency.

Examples in C++:

Factory Pattern: Provides a flexible way to create objects without specifying the exact class, making it easier to add new types of objects without modifying existing code.

Singleton Pattern: Ensures that a class has only one instance, which is useful for managing resources or providing global access to a single object.

Observer Pattern: Defines a one-to-many dependency between objects, so that when one object changes state, all its dependents are notified and updated automatically. This is commonly used in event-driven systems.

Beyond the Code:

Improved Design Thinking: Learning design patterns helps you think more abstractly and strategically about software design. It encourages you to consider different approaches and choose the best solution for your specific needs.

Effective Communication: Design patterns provide a common language for discussing and documenting design decisions, facilitating communication among developers.

In Summary:

Design patterns in C++ are essential for:

Solving common problems efficiently

Improving code readability and maintainability

Promoting best practices and code reusability

Enhancing design thinking and communication

By incorporating design patterns into your C++ development process, you can create high-quality, robust, and maintainable software that meets the demands of modern applications.

Chapter 2

C++ Basics for Object-Oriented Programming

2.1 Classes, Objects, and Methods

Let's dive into the core building blocks of object-oriented programming in C++: classes, objects, and methods. Think of these as the essential ingredients for creating well-structured and reusable code.

Classes: The Blueprint

Imagine you're building a house. You wouldn't start laying bricks without a blueprint, right? In C++, a class is like a blueprint for creating objects. It defines the structure and behavior of a particular type of object.

Data Members: These are the variables that hold the object's data (its attributes or properties). Think of them as the rooms and features of your house.

Member Functions: These are the functions that define what the object can do (its actions or behaviors). Think of them as the doors, windows, and appliances that make your house functional.

Example:

C++

```
class Dog {
public:
  string name;
  int age;
```

```cpp
  void bark() {
    cout << "Woof!" << endl;
  }
};
```

Objects: The Instances

Once you have a blueprint (class), you can create actual houses (objects). An object is an instance of a class, a concrete realization of the blueprint.

Each object has its own unique set of data members, even though they share the same structure defined by the class.

Objects can interact with each other by calling each other's member functions.

Example:

C++

```cpp
Dog myDog;
myDog.name = "Buddy";
myDog.age = 3;
myDog.bark(); // Output: Woof!
```

Methods: The Actions

Methods are the functions that belong to a class. They define the actions that an object can perform.

Methods can access and modify the object's data members.

They can also interact with other objects and perform various operations.

Example:

C++

```cpp
void Dog::bark() {
  cout << "Woof!" << endl;
}
```

Key Concepts:

Access Specifiers: `public`, `private`, and `protected` keywords control access to members from outside the class, enforcing encapsulation.

Constructors: Special member functions that are called when an object is created, used to initialize data members.

Destructors: Special member functions that are called when an object is destroyed, used to clean up resources.

Why This Matters:

Classes, objects, and methods are the foundation of object-oriented programming in C++. They allow you to:

Organize your code: Group related data and functions into logical units.

Create reusable components: Define classes that can be used to create multiple objects.

Model real-world entities: Represent real-world concepts and objects in your code.

Build complex systems: Combine objects to create sophisticated applications.

By understanding these core building blocks, you'll be well-equipped to write effective and well-structured C++ programs using object-oriented principles.

2.2 Constructors, Destructors, and Memory Management

In C++, creating and destroying objects involves managing memory, and that's where constructors and destructors play a crucial role. They ensure objects are properly initialized and cleaned up, preventing memory leaks and ensuring program stability.

Constructors: Object Initialization

Think of a constructor as a setup crew that prepares a building for use. It's a special member function with the same name as the class, automatically called when an object is created.

Purpose:

Allocate memory for the object.

Initialize data members to appropriate values.

Perform any necessary setup operations.

Types of Constructors:

Default Constructor: Takes no arguments, provides default initialization.

Parameterized Constructor: Takes arguments to initialize data members with specific values.

Copy Constructor: Creates a new object as a copy of an existing object.

Move Constructor: Moves resources from one object to another (C++11).

Example:

C++

```cpp
class Dog {
public:
  string name;
  int age;

  Dog()  :  name("Unnamed"),  age(0)  {}  // Default
constructor
  Dog(string  n,  int  a)  :  name(n),  age(a)  {}  //
Parameterized constructor
};
```

Destructors: Object Cleanup

Imagine a demolition crew that carefully dismantles a building. A destructor is a special member function with the same name as the class, preceded by a tilde (~), automatically called when an object is destroyed.

Purpose:

Release any resources held by the object (e.g., memory, file handles, network connections).

Perform any necessary cleanup operations.

Example:

C++

```cpp
class Dog {
```

```cpp
public:
  // ... (constructors)

  ~Dog() {
    cout << "Dog object destroyed" << endl;
    // Release any dynamically allocated memory
here, if needed
  }
};
```

Memory Management in C++

C++ provides two ways to allocate memory for objects:

Stack: Objects created on the stack have automatic storage duration. Their memory is allocated when they are declared and deallocated when they go out of scope.

Heap: Objects created on the heap have dynamic storage duration. Their memory is allocated using the `new` operator and deallocated using the `delete` operator.

Constructors and destructors play a vital role in managing heap-allocated objects:

`new` **operator:** Calls the constructor to initialize the object.

`delete` **operator:** Calls the destructor to clean up the object before deallocating its memory.

Why This Matters:

Proper memory management is crucial for writing robust and efficient C++ programs. Constructors and destructors help you:

Prevent memory leaks: Ensure that dynamically allocated memory is released when no longer needed.

Avoid dangling pointers: Prevent accessing memory that has been deallocated.

Initialize objects correctly: Ensure that objects are in a valid state when they are used.

Clean up resources: Release resources like file handles or network connections when they are no longer needed.

By understanding constructors, destructors, and memory management, you can write C++ programs that are reliable, efficient, and free from memory-related errors.

2.3 Essential C++ Features for OOP

C++ provides a rich set of features that support object-oriented programming. Here are some essential ones that are particularly important for understanding and using design patterns effectively:

1. `this` Pointer: Referring to the Current Object

Imagine you're in a room full of mirrors. Each mirror reflects you, but from a different angle. In C++, the `this` pointer is like a mirror within an object – it's a hidden pointer that always refers to the current object.

Purpose:

Accessing the object's own data members.

Calling the object's own member functions.

Returning the object itself from a member function.

Example:

C++

```
class Dog {
public:
```

```cpp
    string name;

    void setName(string name) {
        this->name = name; // "this->name" refers to
the current object's name
    }
};
```

2. Access Specifiers: Controlling Access to Members

Think of access specifiers as gatekeepers that control who can enter different parts of a building. In C++, they determine the visibility and accessibility of class members (data and functions).

Types of Access Specifiers:

`public`: Members are accessible from anywhere.

`private`: Members are accessible only within the class itself.

`protected`: Members are accessible within the class and its derived classes (we'll discuss inheritance later).

Example:

C++

```cpp
class BankAccount {
private:
    double balance; // Balance is protected from
direct access

public:
    void deposit(double amount);
    double getBalance();
};
```

3. Friend Functions and Classes: Granting Special Access

Sometimes, you need to grant specific functions or classes access to private members of another class. That's where `friend` comes in.

Purpose:

Allowing external functions or classes to access private members of a class, while still maintaining encapsulation.

Example:

C++

```
class MyClass {
private:
    int data;
friend void myFriendFunction(MyClass& obj); //
myFriendFunction can access data
};
```

4. Operator Overloading: Customizing Operators for Your Classes

C++ allows you to redefine the behavior of operators (like +, -, *, /, ==, <, >) for your own classes. This makes your objects behave more like built-in types.

Purpose:

Making your classes more intuitive and user-friendly.

Enabling operations that make sense for your objects (e.g., adding two complex numbers).

Example:

C++

```cpp
class Complex {
public:
  double real, imag;

  Complex operator+(const Complex& other) const {
      return Complex(real + other.real, imag +
other.imag);
  }
};
```

5. Static Members: Shared Resources

Static members belong to the class itself, not to individual objects. They are shared among all objects of that class.

Purpose:

Creating class-level variables or functions.

Keeping track of data that's common to all objects of the class.

Example:

C++

```cpp
class Counter {
public:
   static int count; // Shared counter among all
Counter objects

  Counter() {
    count++;
  }
```

```
};

int Counter::count = 0; // Initialize static
member
```

Why These Features Matter:

These C++ features are essential for effective object-oriented programming. They help you:

Encapsulate data and protect it from accidental modification.

Control access to members and ensure code integrity.

Write flexible and reusable code.

Customize the behavior of your classes.

Manage shared resources efficiently.

By mastering these features, you'll be well-equipped to write robust, maintainable, and elegant C++ code using object-oriented principles and design patterns.

Chapter 3

Inheritance and Polymorphism in C++

3.1 Types of Inheritance in C++

Inheritance is one of the cornerstones of object-oriented programming. It allows you to create a hierarchy of classes, where new classes (derived classes) inherit properties and behaviors from existing ones (base classes). This promotes code reuse, reduces redundancy, and allows you to model real-world relationships.

C++ supports several types of inheritance, each with its own characteristics and use cases:

1. Single Inheritance: A Direct Lineage

Think of single inheritance as a parent-child relationship. A derived class inherits from a single base class.

Characteristics:

Simple and straightforward.

Easy to understand and implement.

Promotes code reuse and specialization.

Example:

C++

```
class Animal { // Base class

public:

    void eat() { cout << "Animal is eating" <<
endl; }

};


class Dog : public Animal { // Derived class

public:

    void bark() { cout << "Woof!" << endl; }

};
```

2. Multiple Inheritance: Combining Traits

Imagine a child inheriting traits from both parents. In multiple inheritance, a derived class inherits from multiple base classes.

Characteristics:

Powerful for combining functionalities from different classes.

Can lead to complex hierarchies and potential ambiguity issues (e.g., the "diamond problem").

Example:

C++

```
class Flyer {

public:

    void fly() { cout << "Flying..." << endl; }
```

```cpp
};

class Swimmer {
public:
  void swim() { cout << "Swimming..." << endl; }
};

class Duck : public Flyer, public Swimmer { // Inherits from both
public:
  void quack() { cout << "Quack!" << endl; }
};
```

3. Multilevel Inheritance: A Chain of Relationships

Think of a family tree with grandparents, parents, and children. In multilevel inheritance, a derived class inherits from another derived class, creating a chain of inheritance.

Characteristics:

Creates a hierarchy of classes with increasing specialization.

Can model complex relationships and hierarchies.

Example:

C++

```cpp
class Vehicle { // Base class
```

```cpp
public:

    void start() { cout << "Vehicle started" <<
endl; }

};


class Car : public Vehicle { // Derived class 1
public:

   void accelerate() { cout << "Car accelerating"
<< endl; }

};


class SportsCar : public Car { // Derived class 2
public:

    void turboBoost() { cout << "Turbo boost
engaged!" << endl; }

};
```

Choosing the Right Type of Inheritance:

The choice of inheritance type depends on the specific needs of your program and the relationships you want to model. Consider the following factors:

Complexity: Single inheritance is the simplest, while multiple inheritance can become complex.

Code Reusability: All types of inheritance promote code reuse, but multilevel inheritance can be particularly effective for creating specialized classes.

Relationship Modeling: Choose the inheritance type that best reflects the real-world relationships between your classes.

By understanding the different types of inheritance in C++, you can create well-structured and maintainable code that effectively models the relationships between your objects.

3.2 Virtual Functions and Abstract Classes

Virtual functions and abstract classes are powerful tools in C++ that enable polymorphism, a key principle of object-oriented programming. They allow you to write flexible and extensible code that can work with objects of different classes through a common interface.

Virtual Functions: Enabling Runtime Polymorphism

Imagine a toolbox with different types of screwdrivers. Each screwdriver has a different head (flathead, Phillips, etc.), but they all share the same purpose: to turn screws. In C++, virtual functions are like those screwdrivers – they allow objects of different classes to respond to the same function call in their own specific way.

How they work:

A virtual function is declared in the base class using the `virtual` keyword.

Derived classes can override the virtual function to provide their own implementation.

When a virtual function is called through a pointer or reference to the base class, the actual function called is determined at runtime based on the type of object being pointed to. This is called dynamic dispatch or late binding.

Example:

C++

```cpp
class Shape {

public:

    virtual void draw() { cout << "Drawing a generic shape" << endl; }

};


class Circle : public Shape {

public:

    void draw() override { cout << "Drawing a circle" << endl; }

};


class Square : public Shape {

public:

    void draw() override { cout << "Drawing a square" << endl; }

};
```

Abstract Classes: Defining a Common Interface

Think of an abstract class as a blueprint that defines the essential structure and behavior of a concept, but doesn't provide a complete implementation. It's like a contract that derived classes must fulfill.

How they work:

An abstract class contains at least one pure virtual function.

A pure virtual function is declared with = 0 in its declaration.

Abstract classes cannot be instantiated (you can't create objects of them).

Derived classes must provide concrete implementations for all pure virtual functions inherited from the abstract class.

Example:

C++

```cpp
class Shape {
public:
    virtual void draw() = 0; // Pure virtual function
};


class Circle : public Shape {
public:
    void draw() override { cout << "Drawing a circle" << endl; }
};
```

Why This Matters:

Virtual functions and abstract classes are crucial for:

Polymorphism: Allowing objects of different classes to be treated as objects of a common type.

Code Reusability: Promoting code reuse by providing a common interface for a family of classes.

Flexibility and Extensibility: Making it easy to add new classes and functionalities without modifying existing code.

Design Patterns: Many design patterns rely on virtual functions and abstract classes to achieve their flexibility and reusability (e.g., Strategy pattern, Template Method pattern).

Key Takeaways:

Virtual functions enable dynamic dispatch, allowing the appropriate function to be called at runtime based on the object's type.

Abstract classes define a common interface for a family of classes, ensuring that derived classes provide specific implementations.

By understanding and using virtual functions and abstract classes, you can write more flexible, extensible, and maintainable C++ code that embraces the power of polymorphism.

3.3 Polymorphism in Action: Runtime Binding and Dynamic Dispatch

Let's bring polymorphism to life with a deeper look at how it works under the hood in C++, focusing on runtime binding and dynamic dispatch.

The Power of Flexibility

Polymorphism, meaning "many forms," allows objects of different classes to be treated as objects of a common type. This is incredibly powerful because it enables you to write flexible and extensible code that can adapt to various situations without needing to know the exact type of object in advance.

Runtime Binding: The Decision at the Last Moment

Imagine you have a remote control with a "play" button. This button can be used to play different devices – a TV, a music player, or a game console. The specific action of "play" depends on the device you're pointing the remote at.

Similarly, in C++, runtime binding means that the decision of which function to call is made at the moment the program is running, not when it's compiled. This is achieved through virtual functions.

Dynamic Dispatch: Finding the Right Path

Think of dynamic dispatch as a traffic controller that directs traffic based on the type of vehicle. When you call a virtual function through a base class pointer or reference, the program uses dynamic dispatch to find the correct function implementation in the derived class.

Virtual Table (vtable): Each class with virtual functions has a hidden virtual table (vtable) that stores pointers to the actual function implementations.

Dynamic Dispatch Mechanism: When a virtual function is called, the program looks up the correct function pointer in the object's vtable and calls that function.

Example:

C++

```cpp
class Animal {
public:
    virtual void makeSound() { cout << "Generic
animal sound" << endl; }
};


class Dog : public Animal {
public:
    void makeSound() override { cout << "Woof!" <<
endl; }
};


class Cat : public Animal {
public:
    void makeSound() override { cout << "Meow!" <<
endl; }
};


int main() {
    Animal* animal1 = new Dog();
    Animal* animal2 = new Cat();


    animal1->makeSound(); // Output: Woof! (Dynamic
dispatch to Dog's makeSound)
```

```
    animal2->makeSound(); // Output: Meow! (Dynamic
dispatch to Cat's makeSound)

}
```

Benefits of Runtime Binding and Dynamic Dispatch:

Flexibility: Write code that can work with a variety of objects without knowing their exact type in advance.

Extensibility: Easily add new classes and functionalities without modifying existing code.

Maintainability: Reduce code duplication and make it easier to modify and update your software.

Key Takeaways:

Runtime binding and dynamic dispatch are essential mechanisms for achieving polymorphism in C++.

Virtual functions and vtables play a crucial role in enabling dynamic dispatch.

Polymorphism promotes flexible, extensible, and maintainable code.

By understanding how polymorphism works in C++, you can write more powerful and adaptable object-oriented programs.

Chapter 4

Factory Method Pattern

4.1 Factory Method Pattern

The Factory Method pattern is a clever way to create objects without needing to know the exact class of the object you'll end up with. It's like ordering a dish at a restaurant – you tell the waiter what you want (e.g., "a vegetarian main course"), and the kitchen (the factory) decides the specific dish (the concrete class) to prepare.

The Problem:

Imagine you're writing a program that works with different types of documents (PDF, DOCX, TXT). You might have code like this:

C++

```cpp
if (fileType == "PDF") {

  document = new PDFDocument();

} else if (fileType == "DOCX") {

  document = new DOCXDocument();

} // ... and so on
```

This approach has a few drawbacks:

Tight Coupling: Your code is tightly coupled to the specific document classes. If you add a new document type, you need to modify this code.

Less Flexible: It's harder to change the object creation logic without affecting the client code.

The Solution: Factory Method

The Factory Method pattern introduces an abstract class or interface (the "factory") that defines a method for creating objects. Concrete factories then implement this method to create specific types of objects.

Benefits:

Loose Coupling: The client code interacts with the factory interface, not the concrete classes, reducing dependencies.

Flexibility: You can easily add new object types by creating new concrete factories.

Centralized Object Creation: Object creation logic is centralized in the factory, making it easier to manage and modify.

Example:

C++

```cpp
// Document interface
class Document {
public:
    virtual void open() = 0;
};


// Concrete document classes
class PDFDocument : public Document { /* ... */
};
```

```cpp
class DOCXDocument : public Document { /* ... */
};


// Document factory interface

class DocumentFactory {

public:

    virtual   Document*   createDocument(string
fileType) = 0;

};


// Concrete document factories

class MyDocumentFactory : public DocumentFactory
{

public:

    Document*   createDocument(string   fileType)
override {

    if (fileType == "PDF") {

      return new PDFDocument();

    } else if (fileType == "DOCX") {

      return new DOCXDocument();

    } // ...

  }

};
```

```
// Client code

DocumentFactory*          factory          =          new
MyDocumentFactory();

Document*                 document                    =
factory->createDocument("PDF");

document->open();
```

Key Takeaways:

The Factory Method pattern provides a flexible and extensible way to create objects.

It promotes loose coupling and centralized object creation logic.

It's a valuable tool for building maintainable and adaptable software.

By using the Factory Method, you can write C++ code that is easier to maintain, extend, and test, as object creation is handled in a controlled and centralized manner.

4.2 Variations of the Factory Method

1. Concrete Creator with Default Implementation

The Basics: The Creator class (the factory) is *not* abstract and provides a default implementation for the factory method.

When to Use: This is useful when you have a common or default type of object that's created most of the time, but you still want the flexibility to create other types in subclasses.

Example:

C++

```cpp
class DocumentFactory {

public:

  virtual Document* createDocument() {

      return new DefaultDocument(); // Default behavior

  }

};



class SpecialDocumentFactory : public DocumentFactory {

public:

  Document* createDocument() override {

    return new SpecialDocument();

  }

};
```

2. Abstract Creator with No Default

The Basics: The Creator class *is* abstract and does *not* provide an implementation for the factory method.

When to Use: This forces all subclasses to provide their own implementation, which is useful when there's no sensible default object type, or when you want to enforce that each subclass defines its own creation logic.

Example: (Similar to the main example in 4.1, where DocumentFactory was abstract)

3. Parameterized Factory Methods

The Basics: The factory method takes one or more parameters that influence the type of object created.

When to Use: This adds flexibility when the creation logic depends on external factors or user input.

Example:

C++

```
class DocumentFactory {

public:

    virtual Document* createDocument(string fileType, int permissions) = 0;

};
```

4. Static Factory Methods

The Basics: The factory method is declared as `static`, meaning it belongs to the class itself, not a specific object.

When to Use: Useful when you don't need to subclass the factory or maintain state within it. It provides a simple way to encapsulate object creation.

Example:

C++

```
class Document {

public:
```

```cpp
    static   Document*   createDocument(string
fileType) {

    // ... object creation logic

    }

};
```

5. Hierarchy of Factories

The Basics: You can have a hierarchy of factories, where each factory creates a specific family of objects. This is often used in conjunction with the Abstract Factory pattern.

When to Use: Useful for creating complex systems with multiple related object types.

Important Considerations:

Simplicity vs. Flexibility: Choose the variation that balances simplicity with the level of flexibility you need.

Maintainability: Ensure your factory methods are well-documented and easy to understand.

Testability: Factory methods can make your code easier to test by allowing you to mock or stub out object creation.

By understanding these variations, you can choose the most appropriate Factory Method implementation for your specific needs and design goals in C++.

4.3 C++ Examples: Abstract Factories and Factory Classes

1. Abstract Factory: A Cross-Platform UI Toolkit

Let's say you're building a UI toolkit that needs to work on different operating systems (Windows, macOS, Linux). You want to create UI elements (buttons, windows, etc.) that look and feel native to each platform.

Abstract Factory: `UIFactory` (defines methods like `createButton`, `createWindow`)

Concrete Factories: `WindowsUIFactory`, `MacOSUIFactory`, `LinuxUIFactory`

Abstract Products: `Button`, `Window`

Concrete Products: `WindowsButton`, `MacOSButton`, `LinuxButton`, etc.

C++

```cpp
// Abstract Factory
class UIFactory {
public:
  virtual Button* createButton() = 0;
  virtual Window* createWindow() = 0;
};
```

```cpp
// Concrete Factory (Windows)

class WindowsUIFactory : public UIFactory {

public:

    Button* createButton() override { return new
WindowsButton(); }

    Window* createWindow() override { return new
WindowsWindow(); }

};


// ... (Similar concrete factories for macOS and
Linux)


// Client code

UIFactory* factory;

if (platform == "Windows") {

  factory = new WindowsUIFactory();

} // ...


Button* button = factory->createButton();

button->draw(); // Will draw a button with the
Windows look and feel
```

2. Factory Class: A Document Creation Library

Imagine a library for creating different types of documents (PDF, DOCX, HTML). You want to provide a simple way for users to create documents without knowing the specific classes involved.

Factory Class: DocumentCreator (with static factory methods)

Concrete Products: PDFDocument, DOCXDocument, HTMLDocument

C++

```cpp
class DocumentCreator {
public:
  static Document* createDocument(string type) {
    if (type == "PDF") {
      return new PDFDocument();
    } else if (type == "DOCX") {
      return new DOCXDocument();
    } // ...
  }
};


// Client code
Document* pdfDoc = DocumentCreator::createDocument("PDF");

pdfDoc->save("my_document.pdf");
```

Key Advantages:

Platform Independence: The UI toolkit example demonstrates how abstract factories can create platform-specific objects without the client code knowing the details.

Simplified Object Creation: The document library example shows how a factory class with static methods can provide a clean and concise way to create objects.

Important Notes:

Product Families: Abstract factories are most effective when you have families of related products (like UI elements or document types).

Flexibility: Factory classes and abstract factories make it easy to add new product types without modifying existing client code.

Design Cohesion: Factories help ensure that objects within a family are compatible and work together seamlessly.

By including these C++ examples in your book, you'll provide readers with concrete illustrations of how to apply abstract factories and factory classes in real-world scenarios, solidifying their understanding of these powerful design patterns.

Chapter 5

Singleton Pattern

5.1 Singleton Pattern

The Singleton pattern is a creational design pattern that ensures a class has only one instance and provides a global point of access to it. Think of it like a unique key to a special room – there's only one, and everyone who needs access has to use that same key.

Why Use the Singleton Pattern?

Managing Shared Resources: When you need to control access to a shared resource, like a database connection, a configuration file, or a logging system.

Global Access Point: When you need a single, easily accessible point of access to an object from anywhere in your application.

Ensuring Consistency: When you need to ensure that all parts of your application are working with the same instance of an object, preventing inconsistencies and conflicts.

Implementation in C++

The key to implementing the Singleton pattern is to:

1 Make the constructor private: This prevents external code from creating new instances of the class.

2 Provide a static instance of the class: This creates a single instance that's accessible through the class itself.

3 Provide a static public method to access the instance: This method controls access to the instance and ensures that only one is ever created.

Example:

C++

```cpp
class Database {
private:
  Database() {} // Private constructor
  static Database* instance;

public:
  static Database* getInstance() {
    if (instance == nullptr) {
      instance = new Database();
    }
    return instance;
  }

  // ... other database operations
};

Database* Database::instance = nullptr; // Initialize static member

// Client code
Database* db = Database::getInstance();
```

```
db->connect();  // Access the single database
instance
```

Variations and Considerations

Lazy Initialization: The example above uses lazy initialization, where the instance is created only when it's first accessed.

Eager Initialization: You can also create the instance at program startup.

Thread Safety: In multi-threaded environments, you need to ensure thread safety when accessing the Singleton instance. This can be achieved using mutexes or other synchronization mechanisms.

Meyers' Singleton: A popular technique that uses a static local variable within the getInstance() method to ensure thread-safe initialization in C++11 and later.

Example (Meyers' Singleton):

C++

```
class Database {
private:
  Database() {}
   Database(const Database&) = delete; // Prevent
copy construction
   Database& operator=(const Database&) = delete;
// Prevent copy assignment

public:
```

```cpp
static Database& getInstance() {

    static Database instance; // Guaranteed to be
initialized only once

    return instance;

}


// ... other database operations
};
```

Key Takeaways

The Singleton pattern ensures that a class has only one instance.

It provides a global point of access to that instance.

It's useful for managing shared resources and ensuring consistency.

Consider thread safety and initialization techniques when implementing the Singleton pattern in C++.

By understanding and applying the Singleton pattern, you can write C++ code that is more robust, maintainable, and efficient.

5.2 Thread Safety and Singleton Implementation

You're hitting on a crucial point! Thread safety is essential when implementing the Singleton pattern in a multi-threaded C++ application. Let's break down the challenges and solutions:

The Problem: Race Conditions

In a multi-threaded environment, multiple threads might try to access the Singleton instance simultaneously. If your implementation isn't thread-safe, you could encounter a race condition:

Scenario: Two threads call `getInstance()` at the same time.

Potential Issue: Both threads might see that `instance` is `nullptr` and try to create a new instance, leading to multiple instances being created, violating the Singleton pattern.

Solutions for Thread Safety

1 Mutex Locking

How it Works: A mutex (mutual exclusion) acts like a lock. Only one thread can acquire the lock at a time. Other threads trying to acquire the lock will be blocked until it's released.

Example:

C++

```
class Database {
private:
  Database() {}
  static Database* instance;
  static std::mutex mutex; // Add a mutex

public:
```

```cpp
static Database* getInstance() {

    std::lock_guard<std::mutex> lock(mutex); // Acquire lock

  if (instance == nullptr) {

    instance = new Database();

  }

  return instance;

}
// ...
};


std::mutex Database::mutex; // Initialize the mutex
```

1 Double-Checked Locking

How it Works: This optimization checks the `instance` pointer twice – once before acquiring the lock and once after – to reduce locking overhead.

Important Note: Requires careful implementation to avoid memory ordering issues. Use `std::atomic` for the `instance` pointer and memory barriers if necessary.

Example:

```cpp
class Database {
private:
  // ...
  static std::atomic<Database*> instance; // Use atomic pointer
  static std::mutex mutex;

public:
  static Database* getInstance() {
    Database* tmp = instance.load(std::memory_order_relaxed);
    if (tmp == nullptr) {
      std::lock_guard<std::mutex> lock(mutex);
      tmp = instance.load(std::memory_order_relaxed); // Double-check
      if (tmp == nullptr) {
        tmp = new Database();
        instance.store(tmp, std::memory_order_release);
      }
```

```
    }

    return tmp;

  }
  // ...
};
```

```
std::atomic<Database*>    Database::instance    =
nullptr;
```

```
std::mutex Database::mutex;
```

2 Meyers' Singleton (C++11 and later)

How it Works: Relies on the guaranteed thread-safe initialization of static local variables. This is often the preferred approach in modern C++.

Example: (As shown in the previous response)

C++

```
class Database {

private:

  // ...
```

```cpp
public:

    static Database& getInstance() {

        static Database instance; // Thread-safe
initialization

        return instance;

    }

    // ...

};
```

Key Takeaways

Thread safety is crucial for Singleton implementation in multi-threaded C++ applications.

Mutex locking, double-checked locking, and Meyers' Singleton are common solutions.

Choose the approach that best suits your needs and C++ version.

Always prioritize correctness and carefully consider potential race conditions.

5.3 C++ Examples: Lazy Initialization and Meyers' Singleton

Lazy Initialization

Lazy initialization means that the Singleton instance is created only when it's first needed. This can be useful to improve startup performance if the Singleton is expensive to create or if it might not be needed at all.

C++

```cpp
class Logger {
private:
  Logger() {} // Private constructor
  static Logger* instance;

public:
  static Logger* getInstance() {
    if (instance == nullptr) {
      instance = new Logger();
    }
    return instance;
  }

  // ... logging methods
};


Logger* Logger::instance = nullptr; // Initialize static member
```

Explanation:

The `instance` pointer is initially `nullptr`.

The first time `getInstance()` is called, it checks if `instance` is `nullptr`. If it is, a new `Logger` object is created and assigned to `instance`.

Subsequent calls to `getInstance()` will simply return the existing `instance`.

Meyers' Singleton

Meyers' Singleton is a popular technique that leverages the thread-safe initialization of static local variables in C++11 and later. It's considered a more elegant and efficient way to implement the Singleton pattern.

C++

```cpp
class Settings {

private:

  Settings() {}

  Settings(const Settings&) = delete; // Prevent
copy construction

  Settings& operator=(const Settings&) = delete;
// Prevent copy assignment


public:

  static Settings& getInstance() {

    static Settings instance; // Guaranteed to be
initialized only once

    return instance;

  }
```

```
    // ... methods to access and modify settings
};
```

Explanation:

The `getInstance()` method contains a static local variable `instance`.

C++11 guarantees that the initialization of static local variables is thread-safe. This means that even if multiple threads call `getInstance()` concurrently, the `instance` will be created only once.

The `instance` is created when `getInstance()` is first called and persists for the lifetime of the program.

The copy constructor and copy assignment operator are deleted to prevent accidental copying of the Singleton instance.

Key Advantages of Meyers' Singleton:

Thread-safe: No need for explicit locking mechanisms.

Lazy initialization: The instance is created only when needed.

Concise and elegant: Simple and easy-to-understand implementation.

Choosing Between Lazy Initialization and Meyers' Singleton

C++ Version: Meyers' Singleton is only available in C++11 and later. If you're using an older version, you'll need to use lazy initialization with explicit locking.

Performance: Meyers' Singleton is generally more efficient due to its thread-safe initialization without explicit locking.

Clarity: Meyers' Singleton is often considered more elegant and easier to understand.

By understanding these examples, you can choose the most appropriate Singleton implementation for your C++ projects and ensure thread safety and efficiency in your code.

Chapter 6

Builder Pattern

6.1 Builder Pattern

The Builder pattern is a creational design pattern that provides a flexible and step-by-step approach to constructing complex objects. It's like having a detailed instruction manual for assembling a piece of furniture – you follow the steps one by one to create the final product.

The Problem: Telescoping Constructors

Imagine you're building a `Car` object with many optional attributes (engine, transmission, color, accessories, etc.). You might end up with a constructor like this:

C++

```cpp
Car(Engine* engine, Transmission* transmission, string color,

    vector<Accessory*> accessories, ...) { /* ...
*/ }
```

This can lead to:

Code Bloat: The constructor becomes long and unwieldy as the number of attributes increases.

Difficult Usage: Clients need to provide values for all parameters, even if they only want to set a few.

Maintainability Issues: Adding or removing attributes requires modifying the constructor and all its call sites.

The Solution: Builder Pattern

The Builder pattern separates the construction of a complex object from its representation, allowing the same construction process to create different representations.

Key Components:

Builder: An abstract interface or abstract class that defines methods for building parts of the product.

Concrete Builder: Implements the Builder interface, providing specific implementations for building each part.

Director (optional): Guides the construction process by calling the builder's methods in a specific sequence.

Product: The complex object being built.

Example:

C++

```
// Product (Car)

class Car {

    // ... attributes (engine, transmission, color,
etc.)

public:

    // ... getters and setters

};


// Builder interface
```

```cpp
class CarBuilder {
public:
  virtual void setEngine(Engine* engine) = 0;
    virtual void setTransmission(Transmission*
transmission) = 0;
  virtual void setColor(string color) = 0;
  virtual Car* getCar() = 0;
};


// Concrete Builder
class SportsCarBuilder : public CarBuilder {
private:
  Car* car;
public:
  SportsCarBuilder() : car(new Car()) {}
  void setEngine(Engine* engine) override { /*
... */ }
          void setTransmission(Transmission*
transmission) override { /* ... */ }
  void setColor(string color) override { /* ...
*/ }
  Car* getCar() override { return car; }
};
```

```cpp
// Director (optional)
class CarDirector {
public:
  Car* constructCar(CarBuilder* builder) {
    builder->setEngine(new SportEngine());
                    builder->setTransmission(new
AutomaticTransmission());
    builder->setColor("Red");
    // ... other steps
    return builder->getCar();
  }
};


// Client code
CarBuilder* builder = new SportsCarBuilder();
CarDirector director;
Car* car = director.constructCar(builder);
 // or
//                    builder->setEngine(...);
builder->setTransmission(...);  ... Car*  car  =
builder->getCar();
```

Benefits:

Step-by-Step Construction: Allows you to build complex objects in a controlled and incremental manner.

Flexibility: You can create different representations of the product using the same construction process.

Readability: The construction process is more readable and easier to understand.

Immutability: You can create immutable objects by ensuring that the builder's methods return the builder itself, allowing for method chaining.

Key Takeaways:

The Builder pattern provides a flexible and readable way to construct complex objects.

It separates the construction process from the object's representation.

It's often used when dealing with objects that have many optional attributes.

By using the Builder pattern, you can write C++ code that is more maintainable, flexible, and easier to use, especially when dealing with complex object creation.

6.2 Fluent Interfaces and Builder Design

Fluent interfaces and the Builder pattern often go hand-in-hand in C++ to create a truly elegant and expressive way of constructing complex objects. Let's explore how they work together:

What is a Fluent Interface?

A fluent interface is a way of designing an API that allows you to chain method calls together, making the code read more like a natural language sentence. It focuses on readability and expressiveness.

Method Chaining: The key to a fluent interface is that each method returns the object itself (`*this`), allowing you to chain calls like this:

C++

```
object.method1().method2().method3();
```

The Builder Pattern and Fluent Interfaces

The Builder pattern is a natural fit for fluent interfaces because it involves a step-by-step construction process. By designing the builder's methods to return `*this`, you can create a fluent interface for building your objects.

Example:

C++

```cpp
class Pizza {
  // ... attributes (size, crust, toppings)
public:
  // ... getters and setters
};


class PizzaBuilder {
```

```cpp
private:
  Pizza* pizza;
public:
  PizzaBuilder() : pizza(new Pizza()) {}

  PizzaBuilder& withSize(string size) {
    pizza->setSize(size);
    return *this;
  }

  PizzaBuilder& withCrust(string crust) {
    pizza->setCrust(crust);
    return *this;
  }

  PizzaBuilder& addTopping(string topping) {
    pizza->addTopping(topping);
    return *this;
  }

  Pizza* build() {
    return pizza;
  }
```

```
};


// Client code

Pizza* myPizza = PizzaBuilder()

                        .withSize("large")

                        .withCrust("thin")

                        .addTopping("pepperoni")

                        .addTopping("mushrooms")

                        .build();
```

Benefits of Combining Fluent Interfaces and the Builder Pattern

Readability: The code becomes highly expressive and reads like a natural language description of the object being built.

Reduced Boilerplate: Fluent interfaces can reduce the amount of code needed to configure complex objects.

Improved Maintainability: Changes to the object's construction process can be made more easily without affecting the client code.

Increased Discoverability: Fluent interfaces can make it easier for developers to discover and understand the available options for building an object.

Key Considerations:

Overuse: Avoid overusing fluent interfaces, as they can sometimes make the code harder to debug if overdone.

Naming: Choose method names carefully to create a natural and intuitive flow.

Consistency: Maintain consistency in your fluent interface design across your application.

By combining the Builder pattern with fluent interfaces, you can create a powerful and elegant way to construct complex objects in C++, making your code more readable, maintainable, and enjoyable to work with.

6.3 C++ Examples: Building Objects with Varying Configurations

The Builder pattern truly shines when you need to create objects with many optional attributes and varying configurations. Here are a few C++ examples to illustrate this:

1. Building a Computer

Imagine you're building a computer with various components (CPU, GPU, RAM, storage). Each component can have different options and configurations.

C++

```
// Product (Computer)

class Computer {

  // ... attributes (CPU, GPU, RAM, storage)

public:

  // ... getters and setters

};


// Builder interface

class ComputerBuilder {
```

```cpp
public:

  virtual ComputerBuilder& withCPU(string model)
= 0;

  virtual ComputerBuilder& withGPU(string model)
= 0;

  virtual ComputerBuilder& withRAM(int size) = 0;

   virtual ComputerBuilder& withStorage(string
type, int size) = 0;

  virtual Computer* build() = 0;

};


//         Concrete         Builders        (e.g.,
GamingComputerBuilder, OfficeComputerBuilder)
// ...


// Client code
Computer* gamingPC = ComputerBuilder()

                    .withCPU("Intel i9")

                    .withGPU("Nvidia RTX 4090")

                    .withRAM(32)

                    .withStorage("SSD", 1000)

                    .build();


Computer* officePC = ComputerBuilder()
```

```cpp
.withCPU("Intel i5")

.withGPU("Integrated")

.withRAM(8)

.withStorage("HDD", 500)

.build();
```

2. Creating a House

Consider building a house with various features (rooms, windows, doors, colors, materials).

C++

```cpp
// Product (House)

class House {

    // ... attributes (rooms, windows, doors, colors, materials)

public:

  // ... getters and setters

};


// Builder interface

class HouseBuilder {

public:

  virtual HouseBuilder& withRooms(int numRooms) = 0;
```

```cpp
    virtual   HouseBuilder&   withWindows(int
numWindows) = 0;

  virtual HouseBuilder& withDoors(int numDoors) =
0;

  virtual HouseBuilder& withColor(string color) =
0;

    virtual   HouseBuilder&   withMaterial(string
material) = 0;

  virtual House* build() = 0;

};


// Concrete Builders (e.g., ModernHouseBuilder,
TraditionalHouseBuilder)

// ...


// Client code

House* modernHouse = HouseBuilder()

                     .withRooms(4)

                     .withWindows(10)

                     .withDoors(2)

                     .withColor("White")

                     .withMaterial("Concrete")

                     .build();


House* traditionalHouse = HouseBuilder()
```

```
                                    .withRooms(6)

                                    .withWindows(8)

                                    .withDoors(3)

                                    .withColor("Brown")

                                    .withMaterial("Wood")

                                    .build();
```

3. Generating a Character in a Game

Imagine creating a character in a role-playing game with attributes like name, class, race, stats, and equipment.

C++

```
// Product (Character)

class Character {

    // ... attributes (name, class, race, stats,
equipment)

public:

    // ... getters and setters

};


// Builder interface

class CharacterBuilder {

public:
```

```cpp
    virtual CharacterBuilder& withName(string name)
= 0;

    virtual  CharacterBuilder&  withClass(string
charClass) = 0;

    virtual CharacterBuilder& withRace(string race)
= 0;

    // ... methods for setting stats and equipment

    virtual Character* build() = 0;
};


// Concrete  Builders  (e.g.,  WarriorBuilder,
MageBuilder)
// ...


// Client code
Character* warrior = CharacterBuilder()
                    .withName("Conan")
                    .withClass("Warrior")
                    .withRace("Human")
                        // ... set stats and
equipment
                    .build();


Character* mage = CharacterBuilder()
                    .withName("Gandalf")
```

```
                .withClass("Mage")

                .withRace("Elf")

                        // ... set stats and
equipment

                .build();
```

Key Takeaways:

These examples demonstrate how the Builder pattern allows for flexible and readable construction of objects with varying configurations.

The client code can choose which attributes to set and in what order, creating different representations of the product.

The Builder pattern promotes code reusability and maintainability by separating the construction process from the product's representation.

By using the Builder pattern, you can write C++ code that is easier to understand, modify, and extend, especially when dealing with complex object creation scenarios.

Chapter 7

Adapter Pattern

7.1 Adapter Pattern

The Adapter pattern is a structural design pattern that allows objects with incompatible interfaces to work together. It's like using an adapter to plug a European appliance into an American outlet – the adapter converts the interface of the appliance to match the interface of the outlet.

The Problem: Incompatible Interfaces

Imagine you have a system that uses a third-party library for image processing. This library has a specific interface for loading images:

C++

```
class ImageProcessor {

public:

  void loadImage(string filename);

  // ... other image processing methods

};
```

Now, you want to use a new image library that has a different interface:

C++

```
class NewImage {
```

```cpp
public:
  void load(string filename);
  // ... other image manipulation methods
};
```

Your existing code relies on the `ImageProcessor` interface, and you don't want to modify it to work with the `NewImage` class.

The Solution: Adapter Pattern

The Adapter pattern introduces an "adapter" class that acts as a bridge between the incompatible interfaces. The adapter implements the target interface (`ImageProcessor`) and internally uses the adaptee (`NewImage`) to achieve the desired functionality.

Example:

C++

```cpp
// Adapter class
class ImageAdapter : public ImageProcessor {
private:
  NewImage* newImage;
public:
  ImageAdapter(NewImage* image) : newImage(image) {}

  void loadImage(string filename) override {
```

```
      newImage->load(filename);  // Adapt the load
method

  }

  // ... adapt other methods if needed

};


// Client code

NewImage* newImage = new NewImage();

ImageProcessor*        imageProcessor      =       new
ImageAdapter(newImage);

imageProcessor->loadImage("my_image.jpg");       //
Uses the adapted interface
```

Types of Adapters

Class Adapter: Inherits from both the target and adaptee interfaces. This is only possible when multiple inheritance is supported.

Object Adapter: Contains an instance of the adaptee and delegates calls to it. This is more common and flexible.

Benefits of the Adapter Pattern

Reusability: Allows you to reuse existing code without modifying it.

Flexibility: Provides a way to integrate components that were not designed to work together.

Maintainability: Keeps your code clean and modular by separating the adaptation logic from your main code.

Key Takeaways

The Adapter pattern is a valuable tool for integrating incompatible interfaces.

It promotes code reusability and flexibility.

It helps you keep your code clean and maintainable.

By using the Adapter pattern, you can seamlessly integrate different components and libraries into your C++ projects, even if they have incompatible interfaces.

7.2 Class and Object Adapters in C++

Class Adapter: Inheritance-Based Adaptation

Mechanism: The adapter class inherits from *both* the target interface and the adaptee class. It uses multiple inheritance to combine the interfaces.

When to Use:

When you need to adapt a single, concrete class.

When multiple inheritance is feasible and doesn't introduce complexities (like the diamond problem).

Example:

```cpp
C++

class OldPaymentGateway {
public:
    void processPayment(int amount) { /* ... old payment logic ... */ }
};
```

```cpp
class NewPaymentGateway {

public:

  void pay(double amount) { /* ... new payment
logic ... */ }

};


// Class adapter

class PaymentAdapter : public OldPaymentGateway,
private NewPaymentGateway {

public:

  void processPayment(int amount) override {

    // Adapt the amount (int to double)

        double    adaptedAmount    =
static_cast<double>(amount);

      pay(adaptedAmount); // Call the adaptee's
method

  }

};


// Client code

PaymentAdapter adapter;

adapter.processPayment(100); // Uses the old
interface, but calls the new logic
```

Object Adapter: Composition-Based Adaptation

Mechanism: The adapter class contains an instance of the adaptee class and delegates calls to it. It relies on object composition.

When to Use:

This is the more common and flexible approach.

When you need to adapt multiple classes or an interface.

When multiple inheritance is not feasible or desirable.

Example:

C++

```cpp
class XMLParser {

public:

    void parseXML(string xml) { /* ... parse XML
data ... */ }

};


class JSONParser {

public:

    void readJSON(string json) { /* ... parse JSON
data ... */ }

};


// Object adapter

class JSONToXMLAdapter : public XMLParser {
```

```cpp
private:

  JSONParser* jsonParser;

public:

    JSONToXMLAdapter(JSONParser*    parser)    :
jsonParser(parser) {}


  void parseXML(string xml) override {

      // Convert XML to JSON (hypothetical
conversion)

    string json = convertXMLtoJSON(xml);

     jsonParser->readJSON(json); // Delegate to
the adaptee

  }

};


// Client code

JSONParser* jsonParser = new JSONParser();

XMLParser*        xmlParser        =         new
JSONToXMLAdapter(jsonParser);

xmlParser->parseXML("<data>...</data>"); // Uses
the XML interface, but calls JSON parsing logic
```

Key Differences and Considerations:

Inheritance vs. Composition: Class adapters use inheritance, while object adapters use composition.

Flexibility: Object adapters are generally more flexible, as they can adapt multiple classes or interfaces.

Complexity: Class adapters can introduce complexity with multiple inheritance.

Overheads: Object adapters might have slight overhead due to delegation.

By clearly explaining these two adapter types with C++ examples, you'll help your readers understand the nuances of the Adapter pattern and choose the most appropriate implementation for their specific needs.

7.3 Examples: Adapting Legacy Code or Third-Party Libraries

The Adapter pattern is a lifesaver when dealing with legacy code or third-party libraries that don't quite fit into your modern C++ projects. Here are some practical examples:

1. Adapting a Legacy Authentication System

Imagine your company has an old authentication system with a clunky interface:

C++

```cpp
class LegacyAuthenticator {

public:

    bool authenticate(string username, string password) {

    // ... old authentication logic ...

    }

};
```

You want to use a new, more secure authentication library:

C++

```cpp
class ModernAuthenticator {

public:

  bool login(string email, string hashedPassword)
{

      // ... modern authentication logic with
hashing, salting, etc. ...

  }

};
```

An object adapter can bridge the gap:

C++

```cpp
class         AuthenticationAdapter         :         public
LegacyAuthenticator {

private:

  ModernAuthenticator* modernAuth;

public:

      AuthenticationAdapter(ModernAuthenticator*
auth) : modernAuth(auth) {}


    bool authenticate(string username, string
password) override {
```

```
    // Assume username is the email

    string email = username;

    // Hash the password using the same method as
the modern library

                string    hashedPassword    =
hashPassword(password);

                return    modernAuth->login(email,
hashedPassword);

  }

};
```

2. Integrating a Third-Party Logging Library

You have a system that uses a custom logging interface:

C++

```
class Logger {

public:

  void logMessage(string message, int severity) {
/* ... */ }

};
```

You want to integrate a popular third-party logging library (e.g., log4cpp, spdlog) with a different interface:

C++

```
// Hypothetical third-party logging interface
```

```cpp
class ThirdPartyLogger {
public:
  void writeLog(string message, LogLevel level) {
/* ... */ }
};
```

An object adapter can make them work together:

C++

```cpp
class LoggerAdapter : public Logger {
private:
  ThirdPartyLogger* thirdPartyLogger;
public:
    LoggerAdapter(ThirdPartyLogger*  logger)  :
thirdPartyLogger(logger) {}


    void logMessage(string message, int severity)
override {
    // Map severity to the third-party library's
LogLevel
                    LogLevel       level      =
mapSeverityToLogLevel(severity);
    thirdPartyLogger->writeLog(message, level);
  }
};
```

3. Adapting a Legacy Data Access Layer

Your application uses an old data access layer with a specific interface:

C++

```cpp
class LegacyDatabase {

public:

   UserData* getUserData(int userId) { /* ... */ }

};
```

You want to switch to a new database technology with a different interface:

C++

```cpp
class NewDatabase {

public:

   User* getUser(int userId) { /* ... */ }

};
```

An object adapter can handle the transition:

C++

```cpp
class DatabaseAdapter : public LegacyDatabase {

private:
```

```cpp
    NewDatabase* newDB;
public:
    DatabaseAdapter(NewDatabase* db) : newDB(db) {}

    UserData* getUserData(int userId) override {
        User* newUser = newDB->getUser(userId);
        // Convert User object to UserData object
        UserData* legacyUserData =
convertUserToUserData(newUser);
        return legacyUserData;
    }
};
```

Key Benefits in These Scenarios:

No Need to Rewrite Legacy Code: Adapters allow you to use legacy code without major modifications, saving time and effort.

Smooth Integration of Third-Party Libraries: Adapters seamlessly integrate libraries with different interfaces into your existing system.

Gradual Migration: Adapters can facilitate a gradual migration to new technologies or libraries.

By providing these concrete examples, you'll demonstrate the practical value of the Adapter pattern in real-world C++ development, especially when dealing with legacy systems or integrating third-party libraries.

Chapter 8

Decorator Pattern

8.1 Decorator Pattern

The Decorator pattern is a structural design pattern that lets you attach new behaviors or responsibilities to objects dynamically, without altering their underlying structure. It's like adding toppings to a pizza – you start with a basic pizza (the core object) and then add layers of toppings (decorators) to customize it.

The Problem: Rigid Class Structure

Imagine you're building a coffee ordering system. You have a `Coffee` class with different types (Espresso, Latte, Cappuccino). You want to add options like milk, sugar, and whipped cream, but creating subclasses for every possible combination would lead to an explosion of classes.

The Solution: Decorator Pattern

The Decorator pattern uses a combination of inheritance and composition to add responsibilities dynamically.

Key components:

Component: An interface or abstract class that defines the core object.

Concrete Component: Implements the Component interface, representing the core object.

Decorator: An abstract class that inherits from Component and has a Component object as a member.

Concrete Decorator: Extends the Decorator class and adds specific responsibilities.

Example:

C++

```cpp
// Component interface
class Coffee {
public:
  virtual string getDescription() = 0;
  virtual double cost() = 0;
};


// Concrete Component
class Espresso : public Coffee {
public:
   string getDescription() override { return
"Espresso"; }
  double cost() override { return 1.99; }
};


// Decorator abstract class
class CoffeeDecorator : public Coffee {
protected:
  Coffee* coffee;
public:
  CoffeeDecorator(Coffee* c) : coffee(c) {}
};
```

```cpp
// Concrete Decorators
class MilkDecorator : public CoffeeDecorator
{
public:
        MilkDecorator(Coffee*    c)      :
CoffeeDecorator(c) {}

   string getDescription() override { return
coffee->getDescription() + ", Milk"; }
     double   cost()   override   {   return
coffee->cost() + 0.50; }
};


class        SugarDecorator      :       public
CoffeeDecorator {
   // ... similar implementation ...
};


// Client code
Coffee* espresso = new Espresso();

Coffee*      espressoWithMilk      =      new
MilkDecorator(espresso);

Coffee*   espressoWithMilkAndSugar   =   new
SugarDecorator(espressoWithMilk);


cout                                        <<
espressoWithMilkAndSugar->getDescription()
<< ": $"
```

```
            << espressoWithMilkAndSugar->cost() <<
    endl;

    // Output: Espresso, Milk, Sugar: $2.99
```

Benefits:

Dynamic Responsibilities: Add responsibilities to objects at runtime without affecting other objects.

Flexibility: Combine decorators to create objects with different combinations of responsibilities.

Avoids Class Explosion: Prevents the need to create a subclass for every possible combination of responsibilities.

Open/Closed Principle: Extends the functionality of objects without modifying their existing code.

Key Takeaways:

The Decorator pattern provides a flexible and dynamic way to add responsibilities to objects.

It uses a combination of inheritance and composition to achieve this.

It's a valuable tool for building extensible and maintainable software.

By using the Decorator pattern, you can write C++ code that is more modular, adaptable, and easier to maintain, especially when dealing with objects that can have varying combinations of features or behaviors.

8.2 C++ Examples: Decorating with Inheritance and Composition

The Decorator pattern cleverly combines inheritance and composition to achieve its flexibility. Let's illustrate this with two C++ examples:

1. Window Decorator (Inheritance)

Imagine you're building a windowing system. You have a basic `Window` class, and you want to add decorations like borders, scrollbars, and menus.

C++

```cpp
// Component interface
class Window {
public:
  virtual void draw() = 0;
  // ... other window methods
};


// Concrete Component
class SimpleWindow : public Window {
public:
  void draw() override {
    // ... draw a simple window ...
  }
};
```

```cpp
// Decorator abstract class (inherits from
Window)
class WindowDecorator : public Window {
protected:
  Window* window;
public:
  WindowDecorator(Window* w) : window(w) {}
};


// Concrete Decorators
class      BorderDecorator      :      public
WindowDecorator {
public:
      BorderDecorator(Window*      w)      :
WindowDecorator(w) {}
  void draw() override {
    window->draw(); // Draw the underlying
window first
    // ... then draw a border around it ...
  }
};


class      ScrollbarDecorator      :      public
WindowDecorator {
  // ... similar implementation ...
};
```

```cpp
// Client code
Window* simpleWindow = new SimpleWindow();

Window*        windowWithBorder        =        new
BorderDecorator(simpleWindow);

Window* windowWithBorderAndScrollbar = new
ScrollbarDecorator(windowWithBorder);


windowWithBorderAndScrollbar->draw();        //
Draws a window with a border and a scrollbar
```

Explanation:

WindowDecorator inherits from Window, allowing it to be used wherever a Window is expected.

Concrete decorators like BorderDecorator override the draw() method to add their decoration.

Decorators can be stacked on top of each other, creating a chain of responsibilities.

2. Pizza Toppings (Composition)

Let's revisit the pizza example, but this time, we'll focus on composition.

C++

```cpp
// Component interface
class Pizza {
public:
  virtual string getDescription() = 0;
  virtual double cost() = 0;
```

```cpp
};

// Concrete Component
class PlainPizza : public Pizza {
public:
  string getDescription() override { return
"Plain Pizza"; }
  double cost() override { return 4.00; }
};

// Decorator (uses composition)
class ToppingDecorator : public Pizza {
protected:
  Pizza* pizza;
 public:
  ToppingDecorator(Pizza* p) : pizza(p) {}
};

// Concrete Decorators
class        CheeseTopping       :        public
ToppingDecorator {
public:
        CheeseTopping(Pizza*      p)       :
ToppingDecorator(p) {}
  string getDescription() override { return
pizza->getDescription() + ", Cheese"; }
```

```cpp
    double    cost()    override    {    return
pizza->cost() + 1.00; }
};


//    ...    other    topping    decorators
(PepperoniTopping, MushroomTopping, etc.)


// Client code
Pizza*    myPizza    =    new    CheeseTopping(new
PepperoniTopping(new PlainPizza()));
```

Explanation:

`ToppingDecorator` holds a `Pizza` object as a member.

Concrete decorators like `CheeseTopping` add their topping to the description and cost by delegating to the contained `Pizza` object.

This example demonstrates how decorators can be implemented using composition, even without inheriting from the component class.

Key Takeaways:

Inheritance: Useful when decorators need to add behavior that's tightly coupled to the component's interface.

Composition: More flexible and allows decorators to be used with a wider range of components.

Combined Approach: The Decorator pattern often uses a combination of inheritance and composition to achieve its flexibility and extensibility.

By providing these C++ examples, you'll illustrate the different ways to implement the Decorator pattern and help your readers understand how to choose the most appropriate approach for their specific needs.

8.3 Real-World Applications: UI Enhancements, Stream Processing

The Decorator pattern isn't just a theoretical concept; it has practical applications in various domains. Here are two real-world examples:

1. UI Enhancements

Imagine you're developing a graphical user interface (GUI) framework. You have basic UI elements like windows, buttons, and text fields. You want to add enhancements like borders, scrollbars, and tooltips to these elements without creating a separate class for each combination.

Core Component: `Window`, `Button`, `TextField` classes

Concrete Decorators:

`BorderDecorator`: Adds a border around a UI element.

`ScrollbarDecorator`: Adds a scrollbar to a window or text field.

`TooltipDecorator`: Adds a tooltip that appears when the mouse hovers over an element.

Example:

C++

```
Window* basicWindow = new SimpleWindow();
Window*         borderedWindow         =         new
BorderDecorator(basicWindow);
```

```
Window*      windowWithScrollbar      =      new
ScrollbarDecorator(borderedWindow);


windowWithScrollbar->draw();   //   Draws   a
window with a border and scrollbar
```

Benefits:

Customization: Users can customize the appearance and behavior of UI elements by adding decorators dynamically.

Flexibility: The framework can be easily extended with new decorators without modifying existing code.

Maintainability: The code remains clean and modular, as each decorator is responsible for a specific enhancement.

2. Stream Processing

Consider a system that processes streams of data, such as sensor readings, financial transactions, or social media feeds. You want to apply various operations to these streams, like filtering, transforming, and aggregating data.

Core Component: `InputStream` class that represents a stream of data.

Concrete Decorators:

`FilteringDecorator`: Filters the stream based on certain criteria.

`TransformingDecorator`: Transforms the data in the stream (e.g., converting units, encrypting data).

`AggregatingDecorator`: Aggregates data in the stream (e.g., calculating averages, counting occurrences).

Example:

C++

```
InputStream*      sensorStream      =      new
SensorStream();

InputStream*      filteredStream      =      new
FilteringDecorator(sensorStream,    /*    filter
criteria */);

InputStream*      transformedStream      =      new
TransformingDecorator(filteredStream,          /*
transformation function */);

InputStream*      aggregatedStream      =      new
AggregatingDecorator(transformedStream,      /*
aggregation function */);


// Process the aggregated stream
```

Benefits:

Dynamic Processing: Decorators allow you to dynamically add or remove processing steps from the stream without modifying the core stream handling logic.

Code Reusability: Decorators can be reused for different types of streams and processing tasks.

Flexibility: You can easily create complex processing pipelines by combining decorators in different ways.

Key Takeaways:

The Decorator pattern is a powerful tool for dynamically enhancing the behavior of objects in various domains.

It promotes code reusability, flexibility, and maintainability.

It's particularly useful in scenarios where objects need to be customized with different combinations of features or behaviors.

By showcasing these real-world applications, you'll help your readers understand the practical value of the Decorator pattern and how it can be applied to solve common design challenges in C++.

Chapter 9

Observer Pattern

9.1 Observer Pattern

The Observer pattern is a behavioral design pattern that defines a one-to-many dependency between objects. When one object (the subject) changes state, all its dependents (observers) are notified and updated automatically. This pattern is like subscribing to a newsletter – when there's a new issue (state change), all subscribers (observers) receive it.

Why Use the Observer Pattern?

Loose Coupling: The subject and observers are loosely coupled, meaning they know little about each other. This makes the system more flexible and maintainable.

Event-Driven Systems: Ideal for event-driven systems where objects need to react to changes in other objects without being tightly coupled.

Dynamic Relationships: Allows for dynamic relationships between objects – observers can be added or removed at runtime.

Implementation in C++

1 Subject:

Maintains a list of observers.

Provides methods for attaching and detaching observers.

Notifies observers when its state changes.

2 Observer:

Defines an interface for objects that want to be notified of changes in the subject.

Implements the notification method to react to changes.

Example:

C++

```cpp
// Observer interface
class Observer {
public:
  virtual void update(Subject* subject) = 0;
};

// Subject class
class Subject {
private:
  std::vector<Observer*> observers;
public:
  void attach(Observer* observer) {
    observers.push_back(observer);
  }

  void detach(Observer* observer) {
    // ... remove observer from the list ...
  }
```

```cpp
    void notify() {
      for (auto observer : observers) {
        observer->update(this);
      }
    }


    // ... methods to change the subject's
state and trigger notifications ...
};


// Concrete Observer
class ConcreteObserver : public Observer {
public:
  void update(Subject* subject) override {
      // ... react to the change in the
subject's state ...
    }
};


// Client code
Subject subject;
ConcreteObserver observer1, observer2;
subject.attach(&observer1);
subject.attach(&observer2);


// ... change the subject's state ...
subject.notify(); // Notify all observers
```

Variations and Considerations

Push vs. Pull Model:

Push: The subject pushes the updated data to the observers in the notification.

Pull: The subject only notifies the observers, and they pull the required data from the subject.

Topics or Events: Observers can subscribe to specific topics or events to receive only relevant notifications.

Thread Safety: Consider thread safety if the subject and observers can be accessed from multiple threads.

Key Takeaways

The Observer pattern defines a one-to-many dependency between objects.

It promotes loose coupling and event-driven programming.

It's useful for building systems where objects need to react to changes in other objects without being tightly coupled.

By understanding and applying the Observer pattern, you can create more flexible, maintainable, and scalable C++ applications.

9.2 C++ Examples: Event Handling and Notification Systems

The Observer pattern is a cornerstone of event handling and notification systems in C++. Here are some examples to illustrate its power:

1. GUI Event Handling

Imagine a GUI application with buttons, menus, and other interactive elements. When a user interacts with an element (e.g., clicks a button), an event is generated. The Observer pattern can be used to handle these events efficiently.

Subject: UI elements (buttons, menus, etc.) act as subjects.

Observers: Objects that need to react to UI events (e.g., update data, display a message, perform an action) act as observers.

Example:

C++

```cpp
// Subject (Button)
class Button : public Subject {
public:
  void click() {
    // ... button click logic ...
      notify(); // Notify observers of the
click event
  }
};


// Observer (Dialog Box)
class DialogBox : public Observer {
public:
  void update(Subject* subject) override {
    if (dynamic_cast<Button*>(subject)) {
      // ... display a dialog box ...
```

```
        }
    }
};
```

```
// Client code
Button button;
DialogBox dialogBox;
button.attach(&dialogBox);

button.click(); // Clicking the button will
display the dialog box
```

2. Notification System

Consider a notification system in an application, where users can subscribe to receive notifications about various events (e.g., new messages, friend requests, system updates).

Subject: The notification system acts as the subject.

Observers: Users or components that want to receive notifications act as observers.

Example:

C++

```cpp
// Subject (Notification System)
class NotificationSystem : public Subject {
public:
    void sendNotification(string message,
string topic) {
```

```cpp
    // ... filter observers based on topic
...
    notify(); // Notify relevant observers
  }
};


// Observer (User)
class User : public Observer {
public:
  void update(Subject* subject) override {
    NotificationSystem* notificationSystem =
dynamic_cast<NotificationSystem*>(subject);
    if (notificationSystem) {
        // ... retrieve and display the
notification message ...
    }
  }
};
```

3. Stock Market Monitoring

Imagine a system that monitors stock prices. When a stock price changes significantly, investors who are interested in that stock should be notified.

Subject: The stock monitoring system acts as the subject.

Observers: Investors who want to be notified of price changes act as observers.

Example:

C++

```cpp
// Subject (Stock Monitoring System)
class StockMonitor : public Subject {
public:
    void priceChanged(string stockSymbol, double newPrice) {
        // ... check if the price change is significant ...
        notify(); // Notify observers interested in this stock
    }
};

// Observer (Investor)
class Investor : public Observer {
public:
    void update(Subject* subject) override {
        StockMonitor* stockMonitor = dynamic_cast<StockMonitor*>(subject);
        if (stockMonitor) {
            // ... retrieve the stock symbol and new price ...
            // ... take action based on the price change ...
        }
    }
```

```
};
```

Key Takeaways:

The Observer pattern is widely used for event handling and notification systems in C++.

It allows objects to react to changes in other objects without being tightly coupled.

It promotes modularity, flexibility, and maintainability in event-driven applications.

By including these examples in your book, you'll demonstrate the practical applications of the Observer pattern and help your readers understand how to use it effectively in their C++ projects.

9.3 Variations: Push and Pull Models

The Observer pattern can be implemented using two main variations: the Push Model and the Pull Model. Each has its own trade-offs in terms of efficiency, flexibility, and information transfer.

Push Model

How it Works: The subject "pushes" the updated data to the observers in the notification. The observer doesn't need to actively retrieve the data.

Advantages:

Simplicity: Easier to implement, as the subject provides all the necessary information.

Efficiency: Observers don't need to make separate calls to get the data.

Disadvantages:

Less Flexible: Observers might receive data they don't need, leading to potential inefficiencies.

Tight Coupling: The subject needs to know what data the observers require, increasing coupling.

Example:

C++

```cpp
// Subject (News Publisher)
class NewsPublisher : public Subject {
public:
  void publishNews(string newsContent) {
    // ...
      notify(newsContent);  // Push the news content to observers
  }
};


// Observer (Subscriber)
class Subscriber : public Observer {
public:
    void update(Subject* subject, string newsContent) override {
    // ... process the news content ...
  }
};
```

Pull Model

How it Works: The subject only notifies the observers that a change has occurred. The observers then "pull" the required data from the subject.

Advantages:

More Flexible: Observers can retrieve only the data they need.

Loose Coupling: The subject doesn't need to know the specific data needs of each observer.

Disadvantages:

More Complex: Requires observers to actively retrieve data.

Potential Inefficiency: Multiple observers might request the same data from the subject.

Example:

C++

```cpp
// Subject (Stock Market Data Provider)
class StockMarketData : public Subject {
public:
  void priceChanged(string stockSymbol) {
    // ...

    notify(stockSymbol); // Notify observers
of a price change

  }


    double getStockPrice(string stockSymbol) {
      // ... return the current stock price
  ...
```

```cpp
    }
};


// Observer (Investor)
class Investor : public Observer {
public:
    void update(Subject* subject, string
stockSymbol) override {
        StockMarketData* stockData =
dynamic_cast<StockMarketData*>(subject);
    if (stockData) {
            double price =
stockData->getStockPrice(stockSymbol);     //
Pull the price
        // ... process the price ...
    }
  }
};
```

Choosing Between Push and Pull

Data Needs: If observers need all the updated data, the Push model is simpler. If observers have varying data needs, the Pull model is more flexible.

Performance: The Push model can be more efficient if all observers need the same data. The Pull model can be more efficient if observers need different subsets of data.

Coupling: The Pull model generally leads to looser coupling between the subject and observers.

By explaining these variations, you'll provide your readers with a deeper understanding of the Observer pattern and how to choose the most appropriate implementation for their C++ projects.

Chapter 10

Strategy Pattern

10.1 Strategy Pattern

The Strategy pattern is a behavioral design pattern that lets you define a family of algorithms, encapsulate each one, and make them interchangeable. This pattern lets the algorithm vary independently from clients that use it. Think of it like having a toolbox with different tools (algorithms) for a specific task – you can choose the right tool (strategy) depending on the job at hand.

Why Use the Strategy Pattern?

Flexibility: Change algorithms dynamically at runtime without modifying the client code.

Maintainability: Keeps your code clean and modular by separating algorithm implementation from the client code.

Extensibility: Easily add new algorithms to the family without affecting existing code.

Testability: Makes it easier to test individual algorithms in isolation.

Implementation in C++

1 Strategy: An interface or abstract class that defines the common interface for all algorithms.

2 Concrete Strategies: Implement the Strategy interface, providing specific algorithm implementations.

3 Context: Maintains a reference to a Strategy object and delegates the work to it.

Example:

C++

```cpp
// Strategy interface
class SortingStrategy {
public:
   virtual void sort(std::vector<int>& data) = 0;
};

// Concrete Strategies
class BubbleSort : public SortingStrategy {
public:
  void sort(std::vector<int>& data) override {
    // ... bubble sort implementation ...
  }
};

class QuickSort : public SortingStrategy {
public:
  void sort(std::vector<int>& data) override {
    // ... quick sort implementation ...
  }
};
```

```cpp
// Context

class Sorter {

private:

  SortingStrategy* strategy;

public:

    Sorter(SortingStrategy*   strategy)   :
strategy(strategy) {}

      void    setStrategy(SortingStrategy*
strategy) { this->strategy = strategy; }

      void   sort(std::vector<int>&   data)   {
strategy->sort(data); }

};


// Client code

std::vector<int> data = {5, 2, 9, 1, 5, 6};


Sorter sorter(new BubbleSort());

sorter.sort(data); // Sort using bubble sort


sorter.setStrategy(new QuickSort());

sorter.sort(data); // Sort using quick sort
```

Benefits:

Dynamic Algorithm Selection: Choose the most appropriate algorithm at runtime based on the specific needs.

Code Reusability: Algorithms can be reused in different contexts.

Reduced Conditional Logic: Avoids complex conditional statements for selecting algorithms.

Improved Testability: Each algorithm can be tested independently.

Key Takeaways:

The Strategy pattern encapsulates and interchanges algorithms.

It promotes flexibility, maintainability, and extensibility.

It's useful when you have a family of algorithms for a specific task and need to choose between them dynamically.

By understanding and applying the Strategy pattern, you can write more flexible and maintainable C++ code that can adapt to changing requirements and incorporate new algorithms easily.

10.2 C++ Examples: Runtime Algorithm Selection

The Strategy pattern excels at allowing you to swap out algorithms on-the-fly, adapting your program's behavior without recompiling. Here are some C++ examples to illustrate this:

1. Navigation App with Route Finding

Imagine a navigation app that needs to calculate routes. Different algorithms might be suitable for different scenarios (fastest route, shortest route, avoiding tolls).

C++

```cpp
// Strategy interface
class RouteFindingStrategy {
public:
```

```cpp
  virtual Route* findRoute(Location start,
Location end) = 0;
};


// Concrete Strategies
class        FastestRoute      :        public
RouteFindingStrategy { /* ... */ };
class        ShortestRoute      :        public
RouteFindingStrategy { /* ... */ };
class        AvoidTollsRoute      :        public
RouteFindingStrategy { /* ... */ };


// Context (Navigation App)
class NavigationApp {
private:
  RouteFindingStrategy* strategy;
public:
  // ...


                                        void
setRouteFindingStrategy(RouteFindingStrategy
* strategy) {
    this->strategy = strategy;
  }


  Route* findRoute(Location start, Location
end) {
    return strategy->findRoute(start, end);
```

```cpp
    }
};


// Client code

NavigationApp app;


// User selects "Fastest Route"

app.setRouteFindingStrategy(new
FastestRoute());

Route* route = app.findRoute(startLocation,
endLocation);


// Later, the user selects "Avoid Tolls"

app.setRouteFindingStrategy(new
AvoidTollsRoute());

route      =      app.findRoute(startLocation,
endLocation);
```

2. Compression Algorithm Selection

Consider a file compression utility that supports different compression algorithms (ZIP, RAR, 7z). The user can choose the algorithm at runtime.

C++

```cpp
// Strategy interface

class CompressionStrategy {

public:
```

```cpp
    virtual void compress(string filename) =
0;
};


// Concrete Strategies
class      ZIPCompression      :      public
CompressionStrategy { /* ... */ };
class      RARCompression      :      public
CompressionStrategy { /* ... */ };
class     SevenZCompression     :      public
CompressionStrategy { /* ... */ };


// Context (Compression Utility)
class CompressionUtility {
private:
  CompressionStrategy* strategy;
public:
  // ...


                                       void
setCompressionStrategy(CompressionStrategy*
strategy) {
    this->strategy = strategy;
  }


  void compressFile(string filename) {
    strategy->compress(filename);
  }
```

```cpp
};

// Client code
CompressionUtility utility;

// User selects "ZIP" compression
utility.setCompressionStrategy(new
ZIPCompression());
utility.compressFile("my_data.txt");

// Later, the user selects "7z" compression
utility.setCompressionStrategy(new
SevenZCompression());
utility.compressFile("my_data.txt");
```

3. Game AI with Different Behaviors

In a game, you might have different AI behaviors for enemies (aggressive, defensive, patrolling). The Strategy pattern allows you to switch between these behaviors dynamically.

C++

```cpp
// Strategy interface
class EnemyBehavior {
public:
  virtual void act(Enemy* enemy) = 0;
};
```

```cpp
// Concrete Strategies
class     AggressiveBehavior    :     public
EnemyBehavior { /* ... */ };
class     DefensiveBehavior    :     public
EnemyBehavior { /* ... */ };
class PatrolBehavior : public EnemyBehavior
{ /* ... */ };


// Context (Enemy)
class Enemy {
private:
  EnemyBehavior* behavior;
public:
  // ...

  void setBehavior(EnemyBehavior* behavior)
{
    this->behavior = behavior;
  }

  void update() {
    behavior->act(this);
  }
};
```

Key Takeaways

These examples demonstrate how the Strategy pattern enables runtime algorithm selection, allowing your C++ code to adapt to different situations and user preferences.

By encapsulating algorithms and making them interchangeable, you create more flexible, maintainable, and extensible software.

This flexibility is a key advantage of object-oriented design, and the Strategy pattern provides a structured way to achieve it in your C++ programs.

10.3 Benefits: Maintainability and Flexibility

The Strategy pattern provides significant benefits in terms of maintainability and flexibility, making your C++ code easier to manage, adapt, and extend over time.

Maintainability

Separation of Concerns: The Strategy pattern promotes a clear separation of concerns by decoupling the algorithm's implementation from the client code that uses it. This makes the code easier to understand, debug, and modify.

Reduced Code Duplication: By encapsulating algorithms in separate strategies, you avoid code duplication and promote code reuse.

Simplified Testing: Each strategy can be tested independently, making it easier to identify and fix bugs.

Improved Readability: The code becomes more organized and readable, as the client code focuses on using the strategy rather than implementing the algorithm itself.

Flexibility

Dynamic Algorithm Selection: You can change the algorithm used at runtime without modifying the client code. This allows your program to adapt to different situations and user preferences.

Easy Extension: Adding new algorithms is straightforward – simply create a new concrete strategy that implements the Strategy interface.

Open/Closed Principle: The Strategy pattern adheres to the Open/Closed Principle, which states that software entities (classes, modules, etc.) should be open for extension but closed for modification. You can add new strategies without modifying existing code.

Adaptability to Change: As your application's requirements evolve, you can easily swap out or add new strategies to accommodate those changes.

Example:

Consider the navigation app example from the previous response. If a new route-finding algorithm is developed (e.g., one that considers traffic conditions), you can easily add it by creating a new concrete strategy without modifying the `NavigationApp` class or any existing client code.

Key Takeaways

The Strategy pattern significantly improves code maintainability by promoting separation of concerns, reducing code duplication, and simplifying testing.

It enhances flexibility by allowing dynamic algorithm selection, easy extension, and adaptability to change.

By using the Strategy pattern, you can create C++ code that is not only functional but also easy to maintain, adapt, and extend over time, making it a valuable tool for building robust and scalable applications.

www.ingramcontent.com/pod-product-compliance
Lightning Source LLC
LaVergne TN
LVHW051737050326
832903LV00023B/962